Virginia, My State
Biographies

# A. Linwood Holton, Jr.

By Moira Rose Donohue

Clarke C. Scott, M. A.
Content Consultant

**Content Review, With Special Thanks**
The Honorable Anne Holton & Governor and Mrs. A. Linwood Holton, Jr.

Your State • Your Standards • Your Grade Level

## Dear Educators, Librarians and Parents . . .

Thank you for choosing this *"Virginia, My State"* series book! We have designed this series to support the Virginia Department of Education's **Standards of Learning for Virginia curriculum studies AND leveled reading**. Each book in the series has been written based on *documented facts at grade level* as measured by the ATOS Readability Formula for Books (Accelerated Reader), the Lexile Framework for Reading, and the Fountas & Pinnell Benchmark Assessment System for Guided Reading. Photographs and/or illustrations, captions and other design elements have been included to provide supportive visual messaging to enhance text comprehension. Glossary and Index sections introduce key new words and help young readers develop skills in locating and combining information. We wish you all success in using this *"Virginia, My State"* series to meet your student or child's learning needs!

**Jill Ward, President**

**Publisher**
State Standards Publishing, LLC
1788 Quail Hollow
Hamilton, GA 31811
USA
1.866.740.3056
www.statestandardspublishing.com

**Library of Congress Control Number: 2012931646**

ISBN-13: 978-1-935884-61-3 hardcover
ISBN-13: 978-1-935884-67-5 paperback



## About the Author

Moira Rose Donohue has a Bachelor of Arts in political science from Mississippi University for Women and a Juris Doctorate degree from Santa Clara University School of Law. She was a banking legislative lawyer for 20 years before she began writing for children. Moira is a published author of numerous poems, plays, and articles, as well as two picture books. She loves dogs and tap dancing and lives in northern Virginia with her family.

## About the Content Consultant

Clarke C. Scott holds degrees from Central Michigan University and has 31 years of experience as a classroom teacher, building principal and system-wide administrator. Clarke currently serves as Director of Middle School Education and Lead Director for History with Pittsylvania County Schools in Virginia. He enjoys hiking, kayaking, caving, and exploring Virginia's and our nation's history. He shares his adventures both above and underground with his wife, Joyce, and three grown children.

1 2 3 4 5 – CG – 16 15 14 13 12

# Table of Contents



**Hi, I'm Bagster!** Let's learn about important Virginians.

Linwood Holton was born in the mountains of southwest Virginia.

Time Line

**1923**
Born

# Early Life in Big Stone Gap

Abner Linwood Holton, Jr. was born on September 21, 1923, in Big Stone Gap. Where is Big Stone Gap? It's in the mountains of southwest Virginia. When Linwood was growing up, Big Stone Gap was an important area for coal mining. His father worked for the railroad company that hauled the coal. Most of the people who lived there, including Linwood, were white. But like the rest of Virginia and the South, Big Stone Gap was **segregated**. African Americans had separate areas in public places. Schools were segregated, too. Black students and white students went to separate schools.

Linwood's babysitter, Carrie, was African American. Sometimes she took Linwood and his brother to the movies. Because she was African American, they had to sit high up in a special section. One time, someone called Carrie a mean name because she was African American. Linwood never forgot how upset that made him feel.

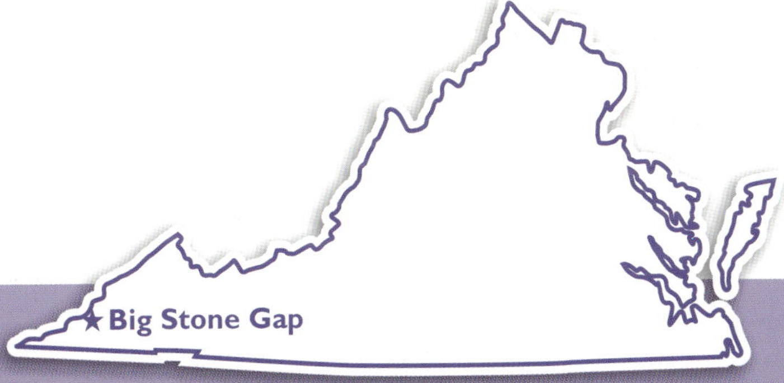

## Big Dreams

Big Stone Gap was a small town. But Linwood had big dreams. "Linwood Holton was running for governor when he was in fourth grade," said a friend years later. Linwood agreed. He thought about being governor a lot. He said, "I can't remember a time when the goal of one day being governor of Virginia wasn't simmering in the back of my mind."

Linwood was very interested in politics. He was also interested in courtroom trials. He became friends with a local **lawyer**. A lawyer represents people in court. Linwood was only a teenager when he helped the lawyer campaign. The lawyer was running for **city council**, but he didn't win. Linwood had his first taste of losing. He didn't know then that there were more losses to come.

Linwood went to Big Stone Gap High School. Today this is Union High School. Linwood liked to ask questions. One of his teachers said Linwood liked to "argue about the answers." This made Linwood a natural for the school **debate** team. Debate teams argue, or debate, about political and social issues. Linwood's team won the state championship his senior year. Debating political issues was good preparation for someone who dreamed of being governor one day.

**Time Line**

**1923**
Born

Linwood was a natural for the debate team at his school, like this one.

Participants in Boys State learn how state and local governments operate.

**Time Line**

**1923** Born

**1941** Goes to college

## Boys State

While Linwood was in high school, he started his own business. He raised chickens from baby chicks. Then he sold the grown chickens to make money. One year, Linwood's high school was invited to send two students to the summer Boys State program in Virginia. Boys State is sponsored by the American Legion. This is an organization for people who have served in the military. The Boys State program is a mock, or pretend, set-up of the state government. For a week, the boys learn how state and local governments operate. They practice running the government, and some are elected to office.

Boys State was the perfect program for someone who wanted to be governor someday, like Linwood. Unfortunately, he didn't get picked to go! Linwood told the principal that he would pay his own expenses if he could go along. He knew he could use money he made from his business. The principal agreed to let Linwood attend the program. Although Linwood wasn't elected governor of Boys State, he was picked to be on the model Supreme Court.

After his Boys State adventure, Linwood returned to school. He graduated from high school and went to college at Washington and Lee University in 1941.

## Never Give Up

Linwood was in college when Pearl Harbor was attacked by the Japanese. Pearl Harbor was a big naval base in Hawaii. The attack brought America into World War II. Linwood wanted to serve his country. The next summer, he signed up to be an officer in the Navy. Linwood was allowed to continue taking college courses. But at the same time, he went to **submarine** school. He graduated from college in 1944. Because he was still in the Navy, his college **diploma** arrived in the mail!

Linwood left the Navy in 1946. He wanted to be a lawyer, like the friend he had campaigned for. Linwood had big dreams. He applied to Harvard Law School in Cambridge, Massachusetts. Harvard Law School is one of the most important law schools in the country. Linwood hoped that he would get in that fall. But he received a letter from Harvard that was not encouraging. The letter said he might not be accepted. Remember how Linwood didn't give up on going to Boys State? He didn't give up this time, either. Linwood asked to meet with the professor who would make the final decision. The professor liked him. He told Linwood to wait until winter to start. This way, he would have a better chance of getting in. Linwood took the professor's advice. He applied to Harvard again, and he got in!

**Time Line**

**1923** Born

**1941** Goes to college

**1947** Enters law school

Linwood went to submarine school during World War II, like these men.

Republicans and Democrats have different ideas about how to run the country, like these 2008 candidates for president.

**Time Line**

**1923** Born

**1941** Goes to college

**1947** Enters law school

**1953** Marries

## Lawyer Linwood

Linwood graduated from Harvard Law School in 1949. He moved to Roanoke, the largest city in southwest Virginia. He applied for a job with a law firm there. But the owners of the law firm didn't want to hire him because he had not gone to law school at the University of Virginia. You know Linwood—he was **persistent**. He didn't give up! He convinced one of the owners of another law firm in Roanoke to hire him.

Soon after Linwood started working for the law firm, he met Virginia Harrison Rogers. Her friends called her Jinks. Jinks worked for the Central Intelligence Agency, called the CIA. The CIA is part of the federal government. It sends spies around the world.

There are two main political parties in the United States. They are the Democrats and the Republicans. They have different ideas about how to run the country. Linwood was a member of the Republican Party. There were not many Republicans in Virginia then. Most Virginia Republicans lived in the southwest, like Linwood, or in the Shenandoah Valley. Almost everyone else in Virginia was a member of the Democratic Party. Linwood's new girlfriend, Jinks, was a Democrat, too. Even so, Jinks and Linwood got married in 1953. She later became a Republican.

## Massive Resistance

In 1954, Linwood opened his own law firm. At that time, many African Americans were actively fighting to stop segregation. This was part of the **civil rights movement**. That same year, the U. S. Supreme Court decided the case of *Brown v. Board of Education*. The *Brown* case made it illegal for public schools to be segregated. The schools now had to **desegregate**. Black students and white students would go to school together.

Many white Virginians did not want **integrated** schools. Senator Harry F. Byrd, Sr. called for a **Massive Resistance Movement**. Byrd and other Democrats told Virginians not to follow the new law. He told them to "resist" integration. Linwood disagreed. He and other Republicans wanted the schools to become integrated over time. However, Governor Thomas B. Stanley, a Democrat, said he would close any public school that tried to desegregate. The next governor, J. Lindsay Almond, followed this plan. He closed several schools in Front Royal, Charlottesville, Norfolk, and Prince Edward County. But soon a federal court said Stanley's plan was illegal. So Almond came up with another plan. He said that students could choose for themselves which school to go to. But only a few students chose to go to integrated schools. Schools in Virginia remained mostly segregated for a long time.



**Time Line**

**1923** Born

**1941** Goes to college

**1947** Enters law school

**1953** Marries

**1954** Opens law firm

Many African Americans were fighting to stop segregation.

Linwood wanted to serve in the Virginia House of Delegates, like these men and women today.

**Time Line**

| 1923 | 1941 | 1947 | 1953 | 1954 |
|---|---|---|---|---|
| Born | Goes to college | Enters law school | Marries | Opens law firm |

# Two-Time Loser

Linwood continued to build the Republican Party in Virginia. He wanted to serve in the state **legislature**, where laws are made. In 1955, he ran for the Virginia House of Delegates. It was a very close race. Linwood lost by only 340 votes. He ran again in 1957. The Republican Party did not support the Massive Resistance Movement, but the party was growing more popular in Virginia. Linwood thought he could win the election. But President Dwight Eisenhower, a Republican, took a stand for desegregation in Little Rock, Arkansas. He sent in troops to force one school to accept black students. Many people all over the country became angry about this, but Linwood supported the president. Just before election day, he took out a big ad in the local newspaper telling people to keep the schools open. He felt it was the right thing to do, even if it hurt his chances of winning. Unfortunately, Linwood's ad upset some Virginia voters and he lost the election.

During this time, Linwood and Jinks had four children: Tayloe, Anne, Woody, and Dwight. Linwood would wake them in the morning and say, "opportunity time!" He saw opportunities everywhere, even when things didn't go his way.

The Virginia state legislature is called the Virginia General Assembly. It is made up of the Virginia House of Delegates and the Senate of Virginia.

## Governor at Last

In 1965, Linwood ran for governor of Virginia against two other people. President Eisenhower remembered how Linwood had lost an election because of what happened in Arkansas. The president did a favor for Linwood. He helped him campaign! The president said, "I expect I owe you one." This time, Linwood came in second. He could have stopped trying. But he thought the first governor's race had been an "opportunity time" for him. It had taught him a lot! Even after three losses, Linwood didn't give up. He ran again in 1969. The president at the time, Richard Nixon, supported him.

Linwood and his family campaigned all over Virginia. Sometimes they traveled in a motor home called "Hi Jinks." Many people appreciated Linwood's stand against Massive Resistance. As his plane landed in Richmond on election night, Linwood learned that he had finally won an election. He had become the first Republican governor of Virginia to be elected in almost 100 years! He had returned the two-party system of politics to Virginia. Because he never gave up, Linwood's boyhood dream had come true. At his **inauguration**, Linwood made it clear that Massive Resistance was over. He promised to unite the state. He said, "For the era of defiance is behind us . . . Let us now endeavor to make today's Virginia a model in race relations."

**Time Line**

- **1923** Born
- **1941** Goes to college
- **1947** Enters law school
- **1953** Marries
- **1954** Opens law firm

Linwood campaigned all over Virginia. President Eisenhower helped him.

**1955 and 1957** Runs for House of Delegates

**1969** Elected governor

Linwood walked his daughter, Tayloe, to her new integrated high school. A member of the capitol police went with them.

**Time Line**

**1923** Born

**1941** Goes to college

**1947** Enters law school

**1953** Marries

**1954** Opens law firm

## Opportunity Time

As soon as Linwood became governor, he put his inaugural speech into practice. His first order was that people would be hired for state jobs fairly. African Americans who applied for state jobs would be treated the same as white people.

That fall, Linwood had another "opportunity time." He and his family were living in the Governor's Mansion in Richmond. The court had ordered Richmond to integrate the schools by **busing** students to schools in other parts of town. Linwood's children were supposed to attend Richmond schools that were now mostly African American. It was Linwood's chance to show people that he meant what he said. On the first day of school, Governor Holton walked his oldest daughter, Tayloe, to her new high school. Meanwhile, Mrs. Holton took their children, Anne and Woody, to their new middle school. Photographers took pictures. One photograph of Tayloe appeared on the front page of the *New York Times* newspaper the next day. It is now famous.

**1955 and 1957** Runs for House of Delegates

**1969** Elected governor

## Changes

Linwood had a lot of work ahead of him. In 1972, he got the legislature to set up the first governor's **Cabinet** in Virginia to help him run the government. He was determined to involve African Americans in the government. Linwood appointed two African Americans to important state jobs. He appointed Bill Robertson, a school principal, to help get more African Americans hired across the state. He also appointed Ernie Fears, a well-known basketball coach, to help run the draft boards in Virginia. These groups decided which young men from Virginia should be required to serve in the military. Fears made sure that African Americans were included on the local boards. Linwood also hired many more women in state government jobs.

Linwood cared about the **environment**. He went to the first Earth Day celebration in Virginia. It was run by students at Virginia Commonwealth University. Virginia did not have an office to look after the environment, so Linwood created one. The new office added two huge state parks: False Cape State Park on the Atlantic coast and Grayson Highlands State Park near Mount Rogers. Linwood promised to clean up the polluted rivers and streams in Virginia, too. He did.



**Time Line**

- **1923** Born
- **1941** Goes to college
- **1947** Enters law school
- **1953** Marries
- **1954** Opens law firm

Linwood helped clean up the polluted rivers and streams in Virginia.

**1955 and 1957** Runs for House of Delegates

**1969** Elected governor

**1972** Sets up Cabinet

Linwood took a new job. He worked with Henry Kissinger, the secretary of state.

**Time Line**

- **1923** Born
- **1941** Goes to college
- **1947** Enters law school
- **1953** Marries
- **1954** Opens law firm

# Next Opportunity

Linwood Holton's term as governor ended in January 1974. By the time he left office, Linwood had increased the number of African Americans working for the state by twenty-five percent. It was "opportunity time" again. He found an opportunity with President Richard Nixon. The president had helped Linwood during his campaign for governor. Now Nixon had a job for him. Nixon asked him to work with Henry Kissinger, the **secretary of state**. The secretary of state helps keep the United States friendly with other countries. Linwood worked to help Congress understand what the secretary of state was doing.

Nixon quit as president later in 1974, and Linwood needed another opportunity. He went back to being a lawyer, this time in Washington, D. C. He tried to run for senator from Virginia in 1978 but didn't get nominated. It would be some time before Linwood had a job in the government again.

**1955 and 1957** Runs for House of Delegates

**1969** Elected governor

**1972** Sets up Cabinet

**1974** Leaves office

## Service to Virginia

In 1986, President Ronald Reagan asked Linwood to manage the airports around Washington, D. C. Within two years, Linwood had made the airports bigger and better.

Linwood Holton's opportunities kept growing. In 1988, he became president of the Center for Innovative Technology. The Center helped create jobs in Virginia. In 2005, he helped with another campaign for governor. This time the candidate was a Democrat named Tim Kaine. But Linwood was a Republican. Why would he help a Democrat run for office? His daughter, Anne, had followed in her father's footsteps. She went to law school at Harvard. She met Tim Kaine there, and they later got married. Like Holton, Kaine went on to be elected governor of Virginia. Now Linwood could visit the Governor's Mansion again. This time, he was there as the father-in-law of the governor.

Remember Linwood's daughter Tayloe, whose picture became famous? She grew up to become a doctor. Anne became a judge. Woody is a history professor and author. Dwight became a lawyer, like his sister and father. He was named after President Eisenhower.

**Time Line**

**1923** Born

**1941** Goes to college

**1947** Enters law school

**1953** Marries

**1954** Opens law firm

Linwood and former governor Douglas Wilder helped Tim Kaine campaign for governor.

**1955 and 1957** Runs for House of Delegates

**1969** Elected governor

**1972** Sets up Cabinet

**1974** Leaves office

Linwood talked about putting his "words to action" in *Opportunity Time*.

**Time Line**

- **1923** Born
- **1941** Goes to college
- **1947** Enters law school
- **1953** Marries
- **1954** Opens law firm

## Words to Action

Linwood Holton believed in the saying, "Actions speak louder than words." He returned Virginia to the two-party system. He helped integrate the state. He hired many African Americans and women in the state government. He cleaned up the polluted rivers in Virginia. He said that being governor was "a great opportunity to set an example of how people ought to behave." Governor Holton put his words to action.

Linwood decided to write a book. He wanted people to hear in his own words what it was like to be governor. You can probably guess what he called the book. It was called *Opportunity Time*. The book was published in 2008. That same year, Linwood became a member of the Southwest Virginia Walk of Fame because of his contributions to Virginia.

**1955 and 1957** Runs for House of Delegates

**1969** Elected governor

**1972** Sets up Cabinet

**1974** Leaves office

**2008** Publishes book

# Glossary

**busing** – Taking students of one race by bus to schools that are attended by students of another race.

**Cabinet** – A group of assistants to the president or governor or other person in charge.

**city council** – A group of officials who make the laws for a city government.

**civil rights movement** – A cause that took place during the early 1960s, where people tried to get equal rights for African Americans.

**debate** – To discuss or argue both sides of a question.

**desegregate** – To abolish, or stop, segregation.

**diploma** – A paper that is the official record of graduation.

**environment** – The type of conditions a plant, animal, or human lives in, including the soil, water, and air around us.

**inauguration** – An official ceremony at the beginning of someone's term of office.

**integrated** – Giving people of all races equal use of public spaces and services.

**lawyer** – Someone who advises people of their rights and represents them in court.

**legislature** – A group of people elected to make laws for a state or country. The legislature in Virginia is called the Virginia General Assembly.

**Massive Resistance Movement** – A policy established to fight the desegregation of public schools in Virginia.

**persistent** – Refusing to give up, continuing a fight.

**segregated** – The separation of people, usually based on race or religion.

**secretary of state** – A government officer who assists the president in relationships with foreign countries.

**submarine** – A boat that sails underwater.

# Index



## Editorial Credits

Designer: Michael Sellner, Corporate Graphics, North Mankato, Minnesota
Consultant/Marketing Design: Alison Hagler, Basset and Becker Advertising, Columbus, Georgia

## Image Credits – *All photos © copyright contributor below unless otherwise specified.*

**4/5** – Courtesy of Southwest Virginia Museum Historical State Park. **6/7** – Classic Stock/Alamy. **8/9** – Andrew Wilds Photography, Lynchburg, Virginia. **10/11** – CORBIS. **12/13** – Charles Dharapak/AP/CORBIS. **14/15** – Bettmann/CORBIS. **16/17** – Washington Post/Getty Images. **18/19** – Campaigning: Waynesboro Public Library Photograph Collection/Library of Virginia; Eisenhower: Courtesy of University of Virginia Press, Charlottesville, Virginia. **20/21** – The *New York Times*. **22/23** – Linda Kloosterhof/iStockphoto. **24/25** – Oath: Courtesy of University of Virginia Press, Charlottesville, Virginia; Kissinger: GYI NSFA/iStockphoto. **26/27** – Morgan Hill, Richmond, Virginia. **28/29** – Book and Holtons: Courtesy of University of Virginia Press, Charlottesville, Virginia.

# Think With Bagster

Use the information from the book to answer the questions below.

1. Linwood talked his principal into letting him go to Boys State. He talked owners of a law firm into hiring him. What words would you use to describe Linwood's personality?

2. Bagster wants to visit Big Stone Gap. Should he bring a bathing suit or hiking boots?

3. Name some "opportunity times" in Linwood's life. Can you name some "opportunity times" in your life?

4. How did Linwood respond to the Massive Resistance Movement? What did this movement stand for? Why did people fight against school desegregation in Virginia? How are things different today?

5. How did Linwood's actions change Virginia? How do these changes affect you today?